Level 1
Early Beginner

# Hachiko

## A loyal dog

Popcorn
ELT
Readers

# Meet ...
## everyone from Hachiko

Hello, I'm Kentaro's dad.

And I'm his mum.

Hi, I'm Kentaro.

Kentaro's dad

Kentaro's mum

Kentaro

**Dr Ueno**

This is Dr Ueno.
Hachiko is his dog.

**Japan**

This is Japan.
Kentaro lives
in Tokyo.

**Tokyo**

I'm Hachiko and I'm
big and brown.

**Statue of Hachiko**

**Hachiko**

**Before you read ...**
What do you think?
Why is there a statue
of Hachiko?

3

# New Words

What do these new words mean? Ask your teacher or use your dictionary.

## fur

The cat has got a lot of **fur**.

## dead

The animal is **dead**.

## house

This is a **house**.

## flowers

He is giving her **flowers**.

## hug

She is **hugging** the dog.

4

## people

There are a lot of **people**.

## statue

The **statue** is very old.

## train station

This is the **train station**.

## wait

They are **waiting** for the bus.

## wolf

The **wolf** is very big and very hungry.

## 'What's wrong?'

What's wrong?

What does the title *Hachiko – A Loyal Dog* mean?
Ask your teacher.

# Hachiko

### *A loyal dog*

## CHAPTER ONE
## 'It's a wolf!'

I am Kentaro. I live in a small house in Tokyo. It's not far from Shibuya train station. I like the station and the big, black trains.

One sunny day, my mum and I go to Shibuya train station. There are a lot of people.

'What time does Dad's train come?' I say.

'At half past five,' says Mum.

Behind the people I see a big, brown and white animal. It has big, brown eyes. Is it a wolf or is it a dog? Is it bad? Is it looking for someone?

'Here's the train!' says my mum.

My dad comes with his friend, Dr. Ueno.

Suddenly, the big animal is next to Dr Ueno.

'It's a wolf!' I say, and I stand behind my mum.

Dr Ueno laughs. 'No, this is my dog. He's a good friend,' he says.

'What's his name?' I say.

'His name's Hachiko.'

Hachiko is a happy dog. I love his long fur.

# CHAPTER TWO
## A sad day

Day after day, I walk to the train station.
The train comes at half past five. Hachiko is
always there too. We wait for my dad and
Dr Ueno.

Sometimes it is very hot, sometimes it is very cold. I give him something to eat and drink and I always hug him.

One day my dad comes from the train, but Dr Ueno is not with him.

My dad is very quiet and sad. 'Dr Ueno is dead, Kentaro,' he says.

That night I go with my dad to the station. It is cold and dark. Hachiko is there. He is looking for Dr Ueno. He is sad. I hug him.

'Here's something to eat,' I say.

'Dad, where is Hachiko living now?' I ask.
'He is with Dr Ueno's brother,' Dad says.
'Please Dad, I want Hachiko here with us!'
'No, Kentaro. Dr Ueno's brother has a
garden and Hachiko can play there.'

Day after day, Hachiko walks for many kilometres to the train station. He waits all day but Dr Ueno never comes.

# CHAPTER THREE
## A good friend

Now I am nine. Hachiko sits and waits for Dr Ueno. People like him very much.

17

I go to see Hachiko a lot. We are good friends now. I always hug him. I love his long fur and brown eyes.

After six years, I see Dr Ueno's brother.

'Hachiko is always at the train station,' I say.

'Yes, he always goes there,' he says.

'Why does he wait after six years?' I ask. 'Dr Ueno is dead. Does he understand?'

# CHAPTER FOUR
## The statue

Now I am sixteen. Hachiko is very old. But day after day, he waits for Dr Ueno.

One morning my mum is
very sad.
'What's wrong?' I ask.
'Hachiko is dead,' she says.

I go to my bedroom and think about Hachiko. I am very, very sad. I want my friend Hachiko, but he is not here now.

I go to the station. There are a lot of flowers for Hachiko. Everyone puts flowers there because everyone in Tokyo loves him.

Now I am an old man. Shibuya station is very big. There is a statue of Hachiko there. People wait there for their friends. They wait next to Hachiko.

There is a special day for Hachiko in April. There are many flowers next to his statue then.

# Real World

# Dogs and people

**Dogs and people can be very good friends.**

Dogs love people. They play with you. Do you have a dog?

1 m

**Great Dane**

65 cm

**Akita**

13 cm

**Terrier**

A **Great Dane** is big! It is one metre (m) tall.

An **Akita** dog is sixty-five centimetres (cm) tall. Hachiko is an Akita dog.

A **Terrier** is small. It is thirteen centimetres (cm) tall. It has lots of fur.

# Dogs help people!

rescue dog

guide dog

Dogs look for people and rescue them.

Dogs look for sheep and other animals.

sheep dog

Which dog do you like? Why?

What do these words mean? Find out.

rescue  guide  sheep  help

# After you read

## 1 True (✓) or False (✗)? Write in the box.

a) Kentaro likes trains. ✓

b) Hachiko is a wolf. ☐

c) It is sometimes cold at the station. ☐

d) Kentaro never hugs Hachiko. ☐

e) People like Hachiko. ☐

f) There is a statue of Dr Ueno. ☐

## 2 Make sentences. Read and match.

a) Dr Ueno is

b) Kentaro gives Hachiko

c) At night Hachiko sleeps

d) Hachiko goes to the station

e) There is a statue of Hachiko

1) for ten years.

2) at the home of Dr Ueno's brother.

3) something to eat.

4) because people love him.

5) a friend of Kentaro's dad.

**Where's the popcorn?**
Look in your book.
Can you find it?

# Puzzle time!

**1 Find and circle six more words in the dog.**

wolf hstationeufuribhappyowfriendnfhugprwait

**2 What trains are the dogs waiting for? Write the sentences.**

Hachiko     Bob     Rex     Sally

**a)** Hachiko is waiting for the half past five train.

**b)** Bob is waiting for the ......................................

**c)** Rex is waiting for the ......................................

**d)** Sally is waiting for the ......................................

## 3 Read the riddles. Find the answers. What is it?

**a)**

It is in **down** and in **bread**.
It is in **old** and in **young**.
It is in **angry** and in **big**.

It's a d __ __ .

**b)**

It is in **far** but not in **car**.
It is in **hungry** but not in **angry**.
It is in **chair** but not in **child**.

It's __ __ __ .

## 4a Read and draw the dog.

My dog is small.
He has long, brown fur.
He has blue eyes.

## b Now draw a picture of a dog and finish the sentences. Read your sentences to your friend.

My dog is ..................... .

He has .................... fur.

He has .................... eyes.

# Imagine ...

## Work with a friend. Act out the scenes.

**A**

**Dr Ueno**: I'm Dr Ueno. What's your name?

**Kentaro**: I'm Kentaro. Is that a wolf with you?

**Dr Ueno** [laughs]:  No, this is my dog Hachiko. He is big but he's not a wolf!

**Kentaro**:  I like his long, brown fur.

**Dr Ueno**:  Yes, he's a happy dog and a good friend.

**B**

**Kentaro**:  Dad, I want Hachiko here in our house.

**Kentaro's dad**: No, he is with Dr Ueno's brother. He has a garden and Hachiko can play there.

**Kentaro**: Can we go to the station and see Hachiko?

**Kentaro's dad**: Yes, we can give him something to eat and drink.

# Chant

**1** Listen and read.

### Hachiko

Love Hachiko,
Hug Hachiko,
See him day after day.

You have always
Got a friend
To run and laugh and play.

When it's hot,
When it's cold,
Hachiko's always there.

Love Hachiko,
Hug Hachiko,
With his long, brown fur.

**2** Say the chant.